Bill Gates

Billionaire Computer Whiz

David Marshall

BLACKBIRCH™
PRESS

THOMSON

GALE

Detroit • New York • San Diego • San Francisco • Cleveland
New Haven, Conn. • Waterville, Maine • London • Munich

For more information, contact
The Gale Group, Inc.
27500 Drake Rd.
Farmington Hills, MI 48331-3535
Or you can visit our Internet site at http://www.gale.com

Photo Credits: Corbis: cover; Ann Ronan Picture Library: 8, 9; Associated Press: 59 (top)/Mike Siegel; Colorific: 21 (bottom)/Marcus Brooke; Gamma: 4–5/Kashi, 16/Kashi, 27/Halstead, 29/Francis Aspesteguy, 41, 42–43/Halstead, 52–53 (main)/Halstead, 58/Francis Apesteguy, 59 (bottom)/Luc Novovitch; Images colour Library: 18, 34–35, 51, 60; image Select: 19, 23 (top), 39 (top); Lakeside School: 12, 13/Rex Ziak, 15 (top), 15 (bottom)/Rex Ziak; Katz: 52 (bottom)/Mcvay/Saba/Rea; Microsoft: 24, 45, 50, 53, 56, 57; Rex Features: 20–21 (main), 21 (top)/Charles Sykes, 47; Spectrum Colour Library: 11/D and J Heaton; Sygma: 7/Joe McNally; Zefa: 23 (bottom)/H.R. Bramaz, 31, 39 (bottom), 40, 46, 48.

LIBRARY OF CONGRESS CATALOGING-IN-PUBLICATION DATA

Marshall, David.
  Bill Gates / by David Marshall.
    p. cm. — (Giants of American industry)
Summary: A brief biography of Bill Gates, best known for his development of Microsoft Windows.
Includes index.
  ISBN 1-4103-0071-4
  1. Gates, Bill, 1955- —Juvenile literature. 2. Businessmen—United States—Biography—Juvenile literature. 3. Computer software industry—United States—Juvenile literature. 4. Microsoft Corporation—History—Juvenile literature. 5. Windows (Computer programs)—Juvenile literature. [1. Gates, Bill, 1955- 2. Businesspeople. 3. Computer software industry. 4. Microsoft Corporation—History.] I. Title. II. Series.

  HD9696.2.U62M37 2004
  338.7'610053'092—dc21

                                                    2003005140

Printed in China
10 9 8 7 6 5 4 3 2 1

Contents

Microsoft on every computer?

Bill Gates had a vision: "A computer on every desk and in every home." His dream was "Microsoft on every computer."

In 1975, nineteen-year-old Bill Gates and his friend Paul Allen founded the computer software company Microsoft. Today, there are few, if any, major industries and commercial organizations that do not rely to some degree on computers. Computer skills have become necessary in almost all jobs, and Bill Gates and Paul Allen had the vision to realize that this would happen.

Gates stated, "The electronic revolution has arrived, full force. And with it has come vast changes in how we work, how we play, how we interact, and even how we think." What Gates did not add when he said this was that he, and his company, had been instrumental in the creation of that revolution.

After just fourteen years, Microsoft became the first software company to sell more than a billion dollars' worth of products in one year. Bill Gates himself, at thirty-one, was the youngest billionaire in American history. By 1994, he had become the richest person in the world.

Gates's vision

In 1993, Bill Gates looked at how Microsoft could develop its future: "As we explore these new directions, we hope to put the raw power of computers to work in new ways, fundamentally improving how technology can serve our customers in their businesses and homes." The essence of Microsoft was to keep on top of developments in technology—often before they were even fully developed—and to sell them to its loyal customers.

Gates applied his knowledge with enthusiasm and drive. The word *workaholic* could have been coined to describe him. He appeared to ignore his personal life and did not seem to care what he looked like to other people. He was not interested in the trappings of success, such as expensive clothes or luxury apartments. Instead, he found more pleasure in making deals. His wealth, he said, simply meant that he no longer had to worry about the cost of what he ordered in a restaurant. Despite the fact that he flew all over the world, he never traveled first class.

As Gates worked his way to the·top, Microsoft sent tremors through the world of computing. When Gates made his forecast about a computer on every desk, the personal computer did not even exist. Nevertheless, Gates had already realized the raw power of computers. He knew that technology could serve customers both in the office and at home. Bill Gates also knew how to make a deal.

Computers

Today it seems obvious to most people that there is a way to tell a computer what to do through what is called a computer language. But in the mid-1970s, nothing about personal computers was obvious. The concept of

computers was a result of the vision and drive of a few gifted people about two hundred years ago.

The origins of the computer date to 1742, when French mathematician Blaise Pascal invented an adding machine. This was refined and developed in the mid-nineteenth century by Charles Babbage, who in 1823 developed a huge "analytical engine" that could actually be programmed. Babbage is credited as the grandfather of computers, yet it was more than one hundred years later, in 1948, that the first true computer was built.

It was not until 1975, though, that the first personal desktop computer, the Altair, was developed for use in the home and office. The computer language that told the Altair what to do was written by two young visionaries named Bill Gates and Paul Allen.

The computer language they developed was named BASIC—Beginners All-purpose Symbolic Instruction Code. Different languages enable computers to perform different tasks. Gates and Allen wanted to use languages to bring computers to the millions of poten-

Led by Bill Gates, pictured here in 1992, Microsoft became the most successful software company in the world.

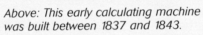

Above: This early calculating machine was built between 1837 and 1843.

Left and right: The Jacquard loom read instructions from a series of punch cards (left). Though they use much-evolved technology, computers today are told what to do in a similar way.

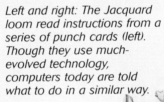

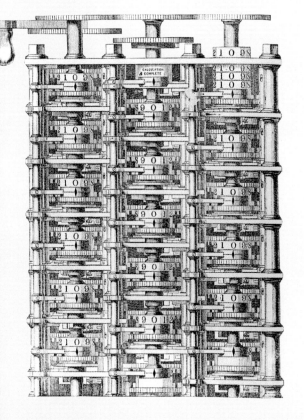

tial customers who were, as yet, unaware of the difference computers were about to make in their lives.

William H. Gates III

William H. Gates III was born on October 28, 1955, in Seattle, Washington. He was born into a wealthy family but never used its money in his own business. His mother, Mary, was a teacher and an important society figure in Seattle who kept Bill organized. His father, known as Bill Jr., was an influential attorney who was strict but supportive with Bill and his sisters, Kristi and Libby.

As a child—and as an adult—Bill was untidy. It has been said that in order to counteract this, Mary drew up weekly clothing plans for him. On Mondays he

might go to school in blue, on Tuesdays in green, and so on. Weekend meal schedules were also planned in detail. Bill always hated to waste time, whether at work or during his leisure time.

Dinner discussions in the Gates family home were always lively and educational. "It was a rich environment in which to learn," Bill remembered.

The Sermon on the Mount

As a boy, Bill seemed fairly ordinary, but in some respects he was very different. When he was eleven, he attended religious confirmation classes where, as a challenge, the minister invited his students to memorize chapters 5, 6, and 7 of the Gospel of St. Matthew in the Bible—known as the Sermon on the Mount. The prize was dinner at the top of the Space Needle, one of the tallest buildings in Seattle.

The Sermon on the Mount is difficult to learn because it is disjointed and repetitive—and very long. When the minister went to the Gates home to hear Bill recite, he was shocked. No one had ever been able to get through the passage without some prompting and many mistakes. Bill simply began at the top and recited the whole passage without a hesitation or a single error. In response to the minister's amazement, Bill said, "I can do anything I put my mind to." This was not a boast—it was just a statement of fact.

A competitive nature

Bill's contemporaries, even during his youth, recognized that he was exceptional. Every year, he and his friends would go to summer camp. Bill especially liked sports and swimming. One of his friends recalled, "He was never a nerd or a goof or the kind of kid you didn't want on your team. We all knew Bill was smarter than us. Even back then, when he was nine or ten years old, he talked like an adult and could express himself in ways that none of us understood."

Bill was also well ahead of his classmates in mathematics and science. He needed to go to a school that challenged him, so his parents decided to send him to

Lakeside—an all-boys school for exceptional students. It was Seattle's most exclusive school and was noted for its rigorous academic standards.

Lakeside allowed students to pursue their own interests. The school's policy was to make conditions and facilities available that would enable all students to reach their full potential. It was the ideal environment for someone like Bill Gates.

Computer access

In 1968, the school made a decision that would change thirteen-year-old Bill Gates's life. Funds were raised, mainly by parents, that allowed the school to gain access to a computer—a program data processor (PDP)—through a teletype machine. If the user typed a few instructions on the teletype machine, the PDP

Above: Bill Gates was born in Seattle, Washington, in 1955.

Opposite top: Gates's mother, Mary (pictured with three-year-old Bill), helped Bill develop organizational skills.

Opposite below: Gates was an excellent student and advanced quickly in school.

11

would send back a response a few seconds later. Bill was immediately hooked. So was his best friend at the time, Kent Evans, and another student, Paul Allen, who was two years older than Bill.

Whenever they had free time—and even at times when they did not—they would dash over to the computer room to use the machine. The students became so single-minded that they soon overtook their teachers in knowledge about computers and got into a lot of trouble because of their obsession. They neglected their other studies, handed work in late, and cut classes. Computer time also proved to be very expensive for the school. The Lakeside teletype machine was connecting by modem to an external mainframe, and time on the mainframe was sold on an hourly basis. Within months, the entire budget that had been set aside for the year had been used up.

Bill Gates (right) and Paul Allen worked on a teletype machine whenever they had a chance while in school.

BASIC and business magazines

At age fourteen, Bill had already begun to write short programs for the computer to perform. He wrote early game programs, such as Noughts and Crosses and Lunar Landing, in what would eventually become his second language, BASIC.

Bill and Paul's fascination with computers and the business world meant that they read a great deal. Paul enjoyed magazines such as *Popular Electronics*, while Bill read business magazines. Computer time was expensive, and because both boys were desperate to get more time and because Bill already saw a way they might succeed financially, the two of them decided to set themselves up as a company: the Lakeside Programmers Group. "Let's call the real world and try to sell something to it!" Bill announced.

First venture

A local computer firm in Seattle, Computer Center Corporation, or C-Cubed, as Bill and Paul nicknamed it, heard about how the Lakeside students had become obsessed with their computer and offered to make a

deal with the school to give it access to its PDP.

The students became even more obsessed. They used all sorts of programs and also crashed—that is, brought down the system—many times. They also ran up huge bills almost immediately. Once, Bill and a couple of his friends broke the computer's security system and found C-Cubed's accounting system. They also found the Lakeside account and reduced the amount of money they owed. Unfortunately for Bill, the company noticed the changes and called the school. Bill was banned from the computer for six weeks.

Bill returned with even greater energy, however. The boys of the Lakeside Programmers Group continued to crash the system and make it completely unusable with increasing regularity. The problem was that when they crashed the system they could no longer pursue their own interests—and neither could C-Cubed's paying customers.

Bill Gates attended the private Lakeside School in Seattle.

. . . .

**"Bugs" in a computer are
a well-known irritation to
all users. They are called
"bugs" because, in 1945,
when an early computer
at Harvard University
failed, an assistant
searched through the
numerous cables and
wires and found that a
large moth had landed in
the workings. This first
computer "bug" was
removed with a pair of
tweezers.**

. . . .

C-Cubed came up with a novel solution to its
problem. It gave the students free computer time in
order to find faults, or bugs, in its software. Computer
software is the term for three different elements: the
operating system, languages, and applications. The
operating system controls the basic functions of the
computer and enables the computer to work, the languages let the user give instructions, and applications
are the computer programs themselves.

The students worked the night shift so that they
would not use the computer during the busy office
hours. All they had to do to get unlimited access to the
computer was make an accurate record of how and
where they found any problems. They would stay up
all night, survive on a diet of soda and pizza, and then
go to school the next day.

Bill Gates's and Paul Allen's devotion and unconventional lifestyle had begun. Like many successful
business people, though, they needed a stroke of
luck—and tremendous dedication—to really get their
business under way.

A year off

At the age of fourteen, Bill was spending days and
nights on end at the computer, so his parents insisted
that he take some time off. He agreed to avoid the
computer room for almost a year to catch up with his
studies. "I tried to be normal," he remembered. He
worked hard and caught up. When the year was over,
though, Bill simply went back to his old routine.

Despite the year off, Bill was a computer guru to
the other students at Lakeside. If anyone at Lakeside
was asked who was the real genius among geniuses,
they named Bill Gates.

The first deal

Despite all the Lakeside Programmers Group's work,
C-Cubed's computer continued to be riddled with
faults. In 1970, C-Cubed failed, and Bill Gates made
the first of many good deals. He also showed how

determined he could be. Without telling Paul Allen and the others, Bill and his friend Kent bought—and hid—C-Cubed's valuable computer tapes. When Paul discovered this, he took the tapes. Bill threatened to sue him if they were not returned, so Paul complied. A little while later, Bill sold the tapes at a profit. Bill had shown that he could cut a deal and ward off any threat to his interests. Even at fourteen, Bill Gates planned to be a millionaire by the time he was thirty.

A payroll program—Bill Gates takes over

In 1971, the Lakeside Programmers Group got its first real business opportunity, although it did not make any money from it. It was asked to write a payroll program for a local company, Information Sciences, Inc. (ISI). Bill was excluded at first, since there was not enough work for the whole group.

The others, however, found it difficult to make any real progress. Eventually, they had to ask Bill to join them. He took charge, and the program was delivered on time. Although ISI had signed a royalty deal with the students, it actually paid the Lakeside Programmers Group in free computer time. They—and Bill in particular—had learned a lot more about how to make deals. Because it was a real business transaction, the Lakeside Programmers Group had to become a formal company. Bill's father, Bill Gates Jr., helped with the legal formalities. He became the new company's principal legal adviser. At the time, Bill Gates and Kent Evans were fifteen years old. "If anybody wants to know why Bill Gates is where he is today, in my judgment it's because of this early experience in cutting deals," recalled Kent's father.

Traf-O-Data

In order to get involved in more deals, Gates and Allen came up with the idea of a system to ease traffic flow in cities—Traf-O-Data. Almost all towns and cities analyzed traffic flow with a system of rubber hoses placed across roads and connected to boxes that contained paper tape that was punched every time a vehicle went over the hose.

Gates and Allen devised a computer program that analyzed the markings on the paper more quickly—and more efficiently—than the usual team of computer analysts could. They also thought they could do the job even more effectively if they had their own computer—so they built one.

It was a great idea, but the computer was never particularly reliable and the desire to build their own computer did not become a driving ambition. It was always important to control the computers they had access to, but Gates and Allen were prepared to let others build the machines. They simply wanted to provide the means to make them work. At this early stage, Bill Gates and Paul Allen were only interested in computer languages.

> "I'm very close to my family. And that's important to me. It's a very centering thing."
>
> —Bill Gates, from the *New Yorker*, January 10, 1994

Opposite: Bill Gates knew that he would become a millionaire from the time he was fourteen years old.

17

Gates and Allen intended to help reduce traffic congestion and air pollution with their computer program, Traf-O-Data.

The Logic Simulation Company

Gates was ambitious and wanted to make better deals and real money even though he was still in school. He formed a different computer group with Kent Evans, called the Logic Simulation Company. In order to expand, they invited other students to join them. They made it clear that they did not just want to recruit "computer freaks" and that there would be equal opportunity for males and females. Gates and Evans wanted the best people available.

In May 1972, the school board asked Gates and Evans to computerize their school's class schedule. Just a week later, however, Kent Evans was killed in a mountain-climbing accident. Despite this shock, Paul Allen joined Bill Gates to do the work. Lakeside School still uses a form of their program for its schedules today.

At age seventeen, Gates was expected to go to the most prestigious university in the United States, Harvard, and graduate at the top of his class. He did, in fact, go to Harvard, but things did not go exactly as planned.

Harvard

At Harvard, Gates found he was not the best student in mathematics. His intention had always been to become a mathematician. Now that he discovered that he would not be the very best mathematician, he did not think it was worth pursuing.

He became known for working at only those problems that challenged him, and he always found the solutions. He also became obsessed with cards. When he was not playing cards, he could be found at a computer. His sleep and work patterns became even more bizarre than when he had worked nights on C-Cubed's computer. He would work for thirty-six hours, sleep for ten, and then start over—even if it was 4:00 A.M.

The computer room was often empty at night—except for Gates. When he became totally exhausted, he would often go to sleep on the tables, only to be woken up by the first class in the morning. He had all the hallmarks of a sterotypical "computer nerd." He was extremely bright, adept at "hacking" (using the computer for entertainment and to access other computers without permission), and had unusual personal habits.

One day, another student found Gates filling in a tax return form. It was a declaration of the profits he had earned from the Traf-O-Data business. None of the other students had even the slightest idea of how to fill in such a form.

One student, Steve Ballmer, was impressed by Gates's intensity and knowledge. He, too, was able to go for long periods without sleep the way Gates could, and he also got very excited when he argued a point. Steve Ballmer became an important friend for Bill Gates.

The Microsoft revolution

If there was one moment that began the Microsoft revolution, it was on a particularly cold December day in 1974 when Paul Allen crossed Harvard Square to visit Bill Gates. Allen had happened to notice the latest copy of *Popular Electronics* magazine. On the cover was a picture of the Altair 8800—a personal computer

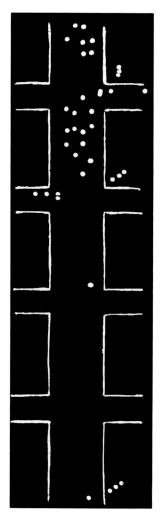

The Traf-O-Data program analyzed data faster and more efficiently than people did. It used images such as the one above, which shows vehicles and traffic lights.

that was sold as a kit in direct competition with commercial computers. Allen saw that this could be the beginning of personal computers that would be available to everyone. He hurried to see Gates, then nineteen years old, and said, "Well, here's our opportunity to do something with BASIC."

Both Gates and Allen realized that the personal computer revolution was about to happen. Gates also anticipated the deals that had to be made if they wanted to get involved in providing the software for these new computers.

*All pictures:
Bill Gates entered
Harvard University
at age seventeen.*

••••••••••••••••••

"I remember
thinking he was
not going to
amount to any-
thing. He seemed
like a hacker, a
nerd . . . with
those glasses, his
dandruff, sleeping
on tables. . . . I
obviously didn't
see the future as
clearly as he did."

—Henry Leitner, a
Harvard classmate

••••••••••••••••••

BASIC

The company that made the Altair computer was called Model Instrumentation and Telemetry Systems (MITS). The owner of MITS, Ed Roberts, needed a simple computer language for the Altair. The simplest language was BASIC, and Gates and Allen told Roberts that they could provide a version of BASIC for the Altair. Gates and Allen knew they needed a routine that would make the computer perform simple basic processes of arithmetic. No one had ever written a BASIC program for a personal computer before.

Roberts did not really believe all the claims. Even so, despite the fact that they did not have the computer, Gates and Allen went to work to create a BASIC program for the Altair 8800 personal computer.

They worked day and night for eight weeks to complete it. They worked with the computer's manual and a diagram of the Altair from *Popular Electronics*. Even without the computer itself, their grasp of the new technology was incredible.

In fact, when Allen went to deliver the BASIC program to Ed Roberts, it suddenly occurred to him in one horrifying moment that they had not written a loader program—a routine that would enable the Altair to actually receive their BASIC program before running it. Allen wrote the loader program off the top of his head, straight onto a piece of paper. Later, when he fed the tape on which the program was written into a tape reader attached to the Altair, it worked perfectly. So did their BASIC program. Gates and Allen were on their way.

"I was dazzled," Roberts remembered. "It was certainly impressive. . . . I was very impressed that we got anywhere near as far as we did that day."

Microsoft is born

The Altair, with its working BASIC, was an amazing breakthrough in computer terms. It was also the single event that caused Microsoft—derived from the words microcomputer software—to be born.

In 1975, Gates and Allen, as Microsoft, officially

Gates and Allen were inspired to develop personal computers after they saw an issue of Popular Electronics *that featured the first minicomputer kit.*

Above: The first
computers took up
entire rooms.

Left: By the 1990s,
microchips such as this
one worked faster and
more efficiently than a
room full of equipment.

signed a deal for their BASIC with MITS. The company goal at that time was to provide languages for the Altair and all the other personal computers that would surely follow. It was the first company specifically formed for this purpose.

Gates, at nineteen, not only understood the complex technology better than almost anyone else, but he also had a grasp of the new legal issues involved in licensing their software. He made sure that the licensing of their BASIC did not depend on the sale of MITS hardware. He granted MITS the right to use and market Microsoft BASIC but did not sell it to them outright. Microsoft kept the ownership of the program regardless of who used or distributed it. In this, Bill Gates set a standard for future software deals.

The PC boom begins

Despite Microsoft's deal with MITS, almost from the moment they met him, Bill Gates and Paul Allen did not get along with Ed Roberts. They had many differences of opinion with him over how to do business, but Allen still went to Albuquerque, New Mexico, where MITS was located, and was hired as MITS's software director. In reality, he was the only software writer there.

The staff at MITS worked all hours to keep up with the phenomenal demand for the first personal computer, the Altair. The *Popular Electronics* article had sparked a public response that was hard to keep up with. It had promised delivery of the Altair computer kit to everyone who ordered one—and within two months. Roberts also demanded BASIC on a diskette— a forerunner of the floppy disk—and Gates and Allen provided it in less than two weeks. Programs stored on the disk could be loaded onto the computer.

Software copying

Gates soon saw that computer fanatics had begun to imitate his and Allen's version of BASIC. He wrote angry letters to computer and electronic magazines. He accused amateurs of stealing. He became well

Gates and Allen created the first computer language, BASIC, for the Altair computer, developed by Ed Roberts's (pictured).

known, but not for the reasons he would have liked. When he was interviewed because of his protests, Gates said he was angry because his company could not get what it deserved from the work it had done.

This was Gates's first real insight into the copying problem that has since plagued the software industry. He made the point that if copying persisted, the money needed to develop new products would simply not be forthcoming—and neither would new software.

Microsoft's first office

Gates and Allen now began to assemble a group of gifted programmers for their new company. They were located in Albuquerque, since Allen was still working for MITS and Bill was officially still a student at Harvard. These unconventional, very intelligent insomniacs became known as the Microkids. Marc McDonald, a twenty-one year old who arrived in Albuquerque in April 1976, was from the Lakeside School computer room. His task was to provide a version of BASIC for the filing system of the National Cash Register Company—one of the two big customers Gates and Allen gained in late 1976. General Electric was the other.

Soon, Allen gave up his job with MITS to work full time for Microsoft. It now looked likely that the company's first year's income would be more than one hundred thousand dollars, and Gates and Allen expected to triple it the following year. Two eminent programmers, Albert Chu and Steve Wood, both twenty-four, arrived to work on development of the language FORTRAN (formula translation), which Gates and Allen believed was the next step for computer languages. As a result of this expansion, Microsoft opened its first offices—four rooms on the eighth floor of a bank building near the Albuquerque airport.

A dropout?

In January 1977, Bill Gates dropped out of Harvard University for good. His parents were alarmed. They were not sure whether he knew what he was doing. After all, no one had become a computer tycoon yet. In fact, most people had never used or even seen a personal computer.

Gates dropped out of college partly because he had become bored with the people there, partly because most of the work did not interest him, and mainly because he was needed in Albuquerque as Microsoft took off. For the next five years, Gates devoted himself exclusively to building the business. Except for two short breaks, he was rarely away from Microsoft—night or day.

Underestimating Bill Gates

One of the first things Gates wanted to do was cancel the agreement with Ed Roberts and MITS. Roberts had said that he would never block a deal Microsoft made to sell its BASIC—unless it was to a competitor of the Altair—and that he would do his best to line up other deals for Microsoft's programs. In 1975, that had not

"... Gates demonstrated a combination of talents that is rare among inventor-entrepreneurs. Besides processing technical skills and expertise, he has also displayed an impressive flair for business."

—From *Scanorama*, September 1993

26

been a problem because there were no other personal computers.

By 1977, however, Commodore had brought out its PET, Tandy had almost perfected its TRS-80, and Apple was emerging with the Apple II. All these hardware manufacturers would need to acquire a version of BASIC—and Microsoft could supply it. It would have to break with MITS to make real money.

Everything came to a head when Roberts sold MITS to another company, Pertec. By this time, the Altair sold in very small numbers. The only real asset MITS had was BASIC—and Bill Gates and Microsoft wanted it back.

When Pertec's lawyers met Gates, they relied on their first impression. They saw a twenty-one year old who looked much younger. Not only did Pertec underestimate him, but the company wrote a letter to Microsoft that said it would no longer market BASIC or allow BASIC to be licensed because Pertec consid-

A relaxed work atmosphere and a casual dress code were adopted by employees in the first Microsoft office in Albuquerque, New Mexico. This attitude is still present in the Seattle-based Microsoft offices (pictured).

ered every other hardware company a competitor. This went completely against Microsoft's old agreement with MITS, and Bill Gates immediately mentioned it to Pertec. As Microsoft's Steve Woods observed, "They came in very arrogant, essentially saying, 'We are this huge multimillion-dollar company and you are just a handful of kids and we are not going to take you seriously.' And that was a big mistake."

Setting the standard

In fall 1977, a court ruled that Microsoft was free to license BASIC. Gates was now free to sell BASIC wherever and whenever he wanted. His natural business sense and foresight had paid off once again.

The money started to flow as Microsoft sold its BASIC to Radio Shack, General Electric, Texas Instruments, Intel, and many others. "Just a plain version of Disk BASIC went for $50,000, and we could make the thing in a couple of hours," one of the programmers recalled.

Microsoft could do it, but hardly any other company at that time had the capacity or knowledge. Certainly no one else had Microsoft's drive to succeed. For the first time, Microsoft began to be the standard for the whole computer industry. Gates said, "We set the standard"—and he meant it.

More contracts

While Allen and the other programmers worked to push the software industry forward, Gates pursued deals with other businesses. He went after original equipment manufacturers—companies that made products that needed a computer in order to function.

Inside every computer-controlled machine—washing machines, car assembly lines, and cash registers, for example—there has to be some sort of computer. Inside every computer there has to be an operating system and a language. As far as Gates was concerned, Microsoft had to sell to all these manufacturers—and it usually did.

He also decided to enter the Japanese market and, in this respect, too, he was well ahead of everyone else. He

could see that Japan would be a major site for computer development. He hooked up with another computer whiz kid with whom he had a lot in common, Kuzuhiko Nishi. Gates and Nishi were about the same age. Both were brilliant, both came from well-to-do backgrounds, both knew how to make deals, and both had dropped out of college to form their own companies.

Nishi formed the ASCII publishing company, which became the largest software company in Japan. He became Gates's eyes and ears in Japan. The one-page agreement they signed in 1977 produced millions of dollars for both Nishi and Microsoft.

Gates dropped out of Harvard in 1977 to pursue his business goals full time.

Work hard, make better products, and win

Now there was no holding Microsoft back. Its growth was nothing short of amazing. Everyone who worked there had a common ideal—work hard, make better products, and win. It was now based in a suite of five offices in Albuquerque with a staff of six. The office doors were all left open and the programmers worked as many hours as necessary to do the job. The pace was frenetic. Gates worked seven-day weeks and often slept on the office floor. The employees extended their hours. No one wanted to be the first to leave. The atmosphere encouraged a relaxed but committed work ethic. Employees wore jeans and T-shirts, not suits, and free soft drinks were provided.

Soon, in order to take care of the administration of the business, a secretary joined the company. Miriam Lubow was appointed when Gates was away on a business trip. When he got back, she protested that "some kid had gone into Mr. Gates's office and was messing with the equipment." It was gently pointed out to her that the "kid" was Gates himself. Lubow became something of a surrogate mother to Gates.

At the end of 1978, Gates and Allen decided that they had to move. Microsoft needed bigger offices because business had boomed. The reason for this success was twofold. First, the Microkids were almost fanatical in the way they worked. It was impossible for them not to work tremendously long hours, because Gates himself did. He never expected anyone to do more than he did, but he did not expect that they would do less, either.

Passionate belief

Gates was, and continued to be, a dynamic business executive. He knew and believed passionately in his product. He believed that it was better to get any deal than no deal at all. He was tireless and worked all hours. He ignored tradition. Because of his zeal and knowledge, his staff always followed his lead.

The personal computer business had exploded. It seemed as if no one could get a computer out fast enough to satisfy consumer demand—and all the computers needed something from Microsoft inside them. By this time, the number of Microsoft employees was up to thirteen and the company had made its first million. In order to expand easily and to be closer

Microsoft's early staff, pictured here in 1978 (with Gates at bottom left), was made up of only eleven members.

to Gates's and Allen's families, Microsoft left Albuquerque and moved to Seattle. Most of the loyal staff chose to go along.

Management style

The early development of Microsoft was fraught with problems over the way Gates, still in his early twenties, handled the rest of the staff. Because he had a short temper and an impatient, confrontational manner, some people found him difficult to work with. His intensity could be seen in the way he rocked back and forth at meetings. He was very hard to satisfy. If groups of programmers worked on a project for weeks, it would not be unusual for Gates simply to say that the result was poor and that they needed to do it again. He always drove those around him at a frantic pace—and he confronted them if he felt they had not done their best work.

When the company moved to Seattle in January 1979, Miriam Lubow was replaced by Marla Wood. At first, Marla was the only member of the office staff. She acted as receptionist, performed all clerical duties, got hamburgers and milk shakes for the programmers, and worked the same hours as the rest of the employees.

Gradually, as the company grew, more secretaries were hired. To Gates, the administrative employees had no technical expertise, and because he had done all the office work himself for years, he underestimated and undervalued their contribution to the company.

The administrative staff members wanted to be paid for all the overtime they were putting in—with back pay. Marla Wood went to her boss to put in the claim. Her boss was also her husband, Steve Wood. He took the claim to Gates, who refused to consider it. Marla and the rest of the administrative staff threatened to take their claim to the state Department of Labor and Industries. Gates thought they were bluffing and told them to try it.

They put in their claim, and Gates was furious. He thought that they were trying to ruin his business. After a short time, they heard that they had won their claim and were paid for their overtime. The amount of money involved was just a few hundred dollars—but the amount of bitterness that resulted was huge.

Gates learned from the experience. He brought in his old friend from Harvard, Steve Ballmer, to be assistant to the president. Ballmer was very similar to Gates in attitude and temperament. They would often argue and get impatient with each other, but the confrontations were always about what was best for the company. Ballmer became an integral part of the Microsoft success story.

Senior staff

The way Microsoft recruited employees demonstrated the intensity of the business and how important it was to get the right staff. Bill Gates believed that Microsoft's success would always be based on the company's ability

. . . .

"Just thinking of things as winning is a terrible approach. Success comes from focusing in on what you really like and are good at—not challenging every random thing."

—**Bill Gates, from the** New Yorker, **January 10, 1994**

. . . .

to attract—and keep—qualified employees.

Almost from the moment he joined the company, Steve Ballmer was Microsoft's recruiting coordinator—although Gates sometimes participated in the recruitment process, too. A high IQ was always essential for someone who wanted to join the company. Almost always, Gates wanted young people straight out of college. Microsoft did not pay particularly well, but it did offer a bustling work environment, free membership to local health clubs, a casual yet committed working atmosphere, and generous opportunities to buy company stock.

The computer is the most important business machine in modern work life. Microsoft focused its software marketing strategy to suit the business world.

The company chose around twenty universities in the United States, Canada, and Japan from which to recruit and went after the most exceptional students. It made personal visits to the colleges and held informal interviews. It asked difficult and bizarre questions to see how the students would react. It posed formidable technical problems and asked interviewees to solve them. In order to succeed at Microsoft, a recruit had to have unlimited drive and enthusiasm. If an interviewee solved the questions and made it through—or better still, enjoyed the pressure of—the interview and had the capacity to look beyond the obvious, then he or she would fit in at Microsoft.

Work hours at Microsoft were completely flexible. Writing programs is creative and intense work, and people need to feel relaxed and motivated. Some people might work a night shift, from 10:00 P.M. to 6:00 A.M. To keep the team atmosphere that Gates and Allen had started, teams of between five and fifteen always worked on specific projects.

IBM enters the personal computer world

In July 1979, Microsoft hired its first marketing director, Steve Smith. He was thirty-four and gave a professional impression. It was important that Microsoft appear credible because it had been approached by the biggest computer company in the world—IBM. If IBM was to continue to dominate the computer industry, it needed to develop a suitable personal computer, one that was small enough for use in the home and versatile enough for use in business.

Gates and Allen were asked to provide both an operating system and languages for IBM's personal computer. Microsoft dealt almost exclusively with languages, such as BASIC and FORTRAN. To take advantage of IBM's business proposal, Microsoft would have to develop operating systems as well.

Microsoft moves into operating systems

Anyone who needed a particular software application for their computer could get it based on the language that Microsoft had already written for that machine. Each machine, however, could have any number of operating systems, and it was a great nuisance to Microsoft's programmers that there were so many systems in the new computers. It meant that every time they sat down at a new machine, they had to modify BASIC for that machine's system. It would have been very helpful to Microsoft if all the machines had the same operating system.

To try to reduce this problem, whenever Microsoft was approached by a client who wanted to buy a new computer setup, Microsoft recommended that the client get in touch with Gates's longtime friend from his C-Cubed days, Gary Kildall. Microsoft would use Kildall's operating system, and in return, Kildall would recommend Microsoft to his clients. It was not that Microsoft and Kildall did not want to compete

Stock Options

If a company needs more capital, or cash reserves, it may decide to go public through a listing on the stock market or stock exchange. This means that people from outside the company are allowed to buy shares in that company. Anyone who buys shares becomes a part-owner of that company and is called a "shareholder" or "stockholder." It is only possible to buy shares in an incorporated company. These are firms whose ownership is divided up into millions of shares that are listed on the stock market or stock exchange.

People buy shares to make money from a company's profits and from increases in the value of the business. Those profits are paid out to stockholders as dividends during the year. The dividends are higher when the company makes large profits and lower when profits are down. Higher dividends raise the cash price of the individual shares, if they are sold.

Many companies today have stock-owning plans for their workforce, like the one offered by Microsoft. These are called employee stock ownership plans (ESOPs). Workers get a stake in the success of the company if they own shares in the business. Shares in a private company, held in an ESOP trust, are given a cash value each year by the company's accountants. Worker-shareholders can then decide whether to hold on to their shares or sell them.

with each other. There was just so much work around that there was no time to do it all, and the relationship worked for both companies. It was only when IBM began to consider its move into personal computers that differences between Kildall's and Gates's companies emerged.

IBM wanted to be at the leading edge of personal computing. It planned to invest millions of dollars in its new product and wanted it to be the best. It decided to use the Microsoft BASIC language and all the applications that went with it. Microsoft BASIC worked on the new IBM machines—but the COBOL, FORTRAN, and Pascal languages that IBM had requested from Microsoft did not. In September 1980, Gates told IBM to talk to Kildall about his operating system and how to get these other languages to work on the IBM machines. He even spoke to Kildall to arrange the meeting.

An important turn of events

The chief negotiator from IBM, Jack Sams, later described the meeting with Kildall as a mess. When IBM representatives arrived to meet Kildall, he was not there. Dorothy McEwan, Kildall's wife and the company vice president, was. She refused to sign a nondisclosure agreement that IBM wanted, and the discussions went downhill from there. IBM decided not to go with Kildall.

As a result, IBM was left without an operating system for its new computer. Gates was aware that problems had occurred and he grew anxious over what might happen to this all-important IBM contract. He was appalled that the lack of an operating system might jeopardize his deal. In a series of meetings, IBM instructed Microsoft to get it an operating system quickly. Microsoft immediately agreed.

MS-DOS

If Bill Gates was lucky when the negotiations with Kildall collapsed, then he had incredible good fortune with the operating system. To develop the system from

nothing would be a hugely expensive and time-consuming exercise, yet Gates, in his ambitious way, anticipated that it would take just a year to develop.

He heard, however, that an operating system had already been developed by Tim Paterson at Seattle Computer Products. It was a rough-and-ready system known as 86-QDOS—the Quick and Dirty Operating System.

Under an agreement that Gates put together himself, Microsoft bought the right to use QDOS for just twenty-five thousand dollars—one of the greatest deals ever made in the short history of the computer industry. Microsoft then modified and improved QDOS for IBM. It became MS-DOS—Microsoft Disk Operating System—and Microsoft's passport to greatness.

After two months of secret negotiations, Microsoft proposed that it could provide IBM with four high-level languages for its personal computer—BASIC, FORTRAN, COBOL, and Pascal—as well as its operating system.

The Microsoft-IBM deal

On his way to IBM to finalize the deal, Gates realized that he did not have a tie with him. Rather than go to the meeting without a tie, he stopped to buy one and arrived half an hour late. He decided he was better off late than without a tie.

MS-DOS was licensed to IBM because the computer manufacturer did not have time to develop its own operating system. The contract was nonexclusive, which was a huge mistake on IBM's part, because it meant Microsoft could license its software to other manufacturers as well as to IBM. IBM mistakenly believed that the big money in the future would be in hardware, not software.

Over the following years, IBM's products were cloned more than any other company's. Its personal computers set the industry standard for hardware, but because of IBM's rush to get the computer onto the market, more than 80 percent of the components came from other companies. This made it easier for other manufacturers to copy the computer and produce what are known as IBM compatibles, or clones.

Computer disks, sometimes called floppy disks, allow users to store and transport information easily.

IBM gained nothing from this mimicry—but Microsoft did, because each clone had to have an operating system and therefore had to license MS-DOS. Before he finalized the deal with IBM, Gates had to own the exclusive rights to 86-QDOS. He did not want to be tied to IBM, since he would not have the flexibility to approach others. After very little negotiation, he was able to buy 86-QDOS outright for fifty thousand dollars—a bargain.

When IBM and Microsoft began their relationship in 1980, they were at opposite ends of the business spectrum: IBM had 340,000 employees and annual earnings of $3.6 billion; Microsoft was still only a start-up company with around thirty-two employees and a fairly slim profit margin. Microsoft had Bill Gates, however, and, thanks to him, it also had MS-DOS. Now that the personal computer had an operating system, the number of applications could only grow.

Applications take off

Applications are programs that allow a computer to perform specific functions. For instance, they might turn a computer into a word processor, a machine that can be used like a typewriter but stores information as well. Bill Gates visualized another huge market—and fortune—in applications software. This was to be the third part—along with BASIC, the other computer languages, and the MS-DOS operating system—of Microsoft's business.

In 1981, Gates decided to get Microsoft heavily involved in the applications market. He wanted to write and sell the best word-processing program, the best accounting program, and the best information program, or database. Microsoft was slow to get started in this area, but once it got under way it was dominant. Gates could see that although Microsoft was

Microsoft created the computer language MS-DOS for IBM. Here, Gates displays a disk with a version of that program on it.

Microsoft required hard work from its employees but also encouraged fun and creativity in the workplace.

extremely successful in certain areas, it needed to continue its expansion into other areas in order to secure its place in the market.

In 1982, Ballmer persuaded Gates that they needed a professional manager. Because none of their workforce had ever had any management training, they appointed James Towne from Tektronix. It was a significant choice mainly because it was so inappropriate. Towne was an excellent manager but did not know how to adjust to Microsoft's unconventional atmosphere in which employees worked all hours and lived, ate, and dreamed Microsoft. After eleven months, Gates had to "let him [Towne] go." Gates admitted that it had been a mistake to hire Towne. He would soon lose his founding partner.

Paul Allen leaves

Late in 1982, Paul Allen became seriously ill. Tests showed that he had Hodgkin's disease (cancer of the lymph nodes). After eight years of tough eighty-hour weeks and few, if any, breaks, Allen withdrew partially from Microsoft. In 1983, he decided to leave the company completely. After a while, the disease went into remission. Although he had been less visible than Gates, his dedication and vision had been essential in the creation of Microsoft.

Microsoft Word

Meanwhile, competition in the applications market was heating up. Another software company, Lotus, had launched an accounting program in direct competition with Microsoft's, and this had hurt Gates.

Lotus had gambled that the IBM personal computer would be the standard machine and that everyone would have one. Therefore, it made its accounting program fit the IBM personal computer. The program would not run on any other machine, but because it was just for the IBM, it was incredibly fast. Microsoft's program, on the other hand, was written to work on many other machines, which made it slower. Lotus' risk paid off. It showed how important it is to bring a good product to the marketplace as quickly as possible—a concept that was normally an essential part of Gates's marketing strategy.

In the spring of 1983, Microsoft's Word application was launched as a supposedly quick and powerful word processor. It was hugely successful, and as it was further developed, it continued to improve. It had taken Charles Simonyi, the genius who was at the heart of many of Microsoft's best-selling applications, more than a year to finish Word. Like all of Gates's efforts, Word was designed to make Microsoft more powerful in the marketplace.

A multimillion-dollar launch

The launch of Microsoft Word cost the company around $3.5 million in free offers, magazine promotions, and thousands of handouts. This aggressive sales technique fit in well with Gates's methods. As part of its expansion, Microsoft made Rowland Hanson part of its management team. Before Microsoft, Hanson had sold soap products. He knew very little about computers, but he did know how to sell.

Microsoft already made the best products in the computer software business. Now it had to sell them. Gates needed expert help. Hanson made a simple, but important, decision. He emphasized that it was the name Microsoft that people would look for—and trust—if its products were the best, which Gates insisted they were.

Everyone had heard of Microsoft's rival in the word-processing field, WordStar, but hardly anyone

Paul Allen (left) and Bill Gates ended their partnership in 1983 when Allen left the company for health reasons.

knew the name of the company that produced it. Hanson was determined not to let this happen to Microsoft. If a new product was launched with Microsoft's name on it, customers would expect Microsoft excellence. So every Microsoft product was marketed with the company's name in front of it. Word became Microsoft Word, Excel began as Microsoft Excel, and so on. It made a real difference.

Improvements

There was a problem with Microsoft Word in 1983, though. It was simply not as good as it could have been. It was not until the third version, Microsoft Word 3.1, that the program began to pay for itself and become a leader in its market. Always eager to get into the marketplace as soon as possible, Gates had felt that improvements could be made later. He followed the advice of General George S. Patton that "a good plan, violently executed now, is better than a perfect plan

• • • • • • • • • • • • • • • • • • • •

".. . sometimes customers do express dissatisfaction with one aspect or another of our products or our business, and yes, we hear them and we follow up on their concerns. What's even more important is that we build that knowledge into our operations and planning, reshaping how we do business so those concerns won't arise with other customers in the future."

—Bill Gates, 1993

• • • • • • • • • • • • • • • • • • • •

next week." He believed that while one waited to have a perfect product, the market might well disappear.

Windows

Although Microsoft Word 1.0 was far from perfect, it had one or two new features. The most important was that it had a graphical user interface (GUI). A GUI uses words, pictures, and icons on the computer screen instead of the numbers and letters of a text program. It was designed to make computers easier to use. Bill Gates wanted a computer that had a GUI. It was one of his visions. He wanted to make the computer appear friendly and accessible to the user. When a person switched on a computer, it was intimidating to see just a flashing marker on a black screen. Gates insisted that Microsoft begin work on its own GUI operating system, which would be named Microsoft Windows.

Thirty of the company's best programmers worked two years to develop a product that was very poor at first. Overall, they spent about eighty work years on the design, writing, and testing of Windows. To Bill Gates, however, it was worth the effort. He wanted something that would not only look good and be user-friendly, but would also help users be more efficient. Gates wanted a system that would allow the user to move between different applications easily, and he wanted it to be run with a "mouse." The mouse, also devised to make a computer easy to operate, is a small, handheld unit that, when moved around on a flat pad, moves an arrow called a cursor to the required position on the screen.

Advance product announcements

Gates made deals and kept rivals at bay by announcing the forthcoming release of Microsoft Windows and other products months in advance of their real launch dates. One magazine called these incomplete products "vaporware." These advance announcements encouraged customers, who were made aware that Microsoft was launching a new product in the near future, to wait rather than buy a rival's product sooner. Some considered this practice unfair trading, but it worked for Windows because many of Microsoft's rivals already produced their own GUI applications—and they were ahead of Microsoft.

Gates, however, ran into trouble with IBM, which wanted to launch its own GUI application. He made deals with twenty-four other computer makers in which he stressed that they should support Microsoft Windows rather than the rival IBM application. The relationship with IBM had begun to unravel. IBM was not as influential in the industry as it had hoped. Microsoft was in charge of everything that happened on the IBM personal computer. IBM was losing even on the computer itself because IBM clones now made up at least 60 percent of the computer market.

It was important for IBM to take control once again. It decided that the time was right to produce an

....
"Our success is based on only one thing: good products. It's not very complicated. We're not powerful enough to cause products that are not excellent to sell well."

—Bill Gates, 1993
....

Microsoft Windows 1.0 provided users with a graphical user interface (GUI) intended to make computers easier to use.

updated version of Microsoft's operating system, MS-DOS, and run IBM's own GUI application on it. It was Microsoft's responsibility to update MS-DOS. Gates said he would—but he continued to work on Microsoft Windows as well.

Pressure at Microsoft

Gates worked at a hectic pace and expected the same from those around him. His average workweek was sixty-five hours. When he was not at work, he often read. He loved to read other companies' success stories—and learn from them—along with biographies of great scientists, politicians, and business executives. In the first five years of Microsoft's existence, Gates took only two three-day breaks. In the mid-1980s, he increased that time off to just one week a year, and, to celebrate when Microsoft went public, he even hired a yacht for four days.

Many of those who went to Microsoft followed Gates's work ethic, but the pace at Microsoft had some casualties. One of the senior programmers worked one-hundred-hour weeks—and was subject to Gates's pressure and short temper at the same time. After a few months, he suffered heart failure and had to leave the company. As a senior executive said later, "You are surrounded with people who are very much the same, and the people who run the company are the same, so you just go and go and go. There would be times when people would work more than we wanted them to, and we would try and get them to slow down but sometimes you couldn't get them to stop. When they collapsed you covered them with a blanket and turned off the computer.

"I saw kids, you know, who worked at Microsoft for a few years and truly, I wondered if they would ever be able to work again." If the work schedule did not exhaust employees, Gates's "discussion" technique might do so. It even

Though the first mouse (a button-controlled clicker device) was created in 1963 when Bill Gates was still a child, Microsoft originated the type we know today.

rebounded on Ballmer—Gates's right-hand man. The delays in getting Windows finished were legendary and significant. Influential magazines wrote that Microsoft would never be able to deliver its highly publicized new title. By 1985, Gates had begun to run out of patience and said so—loudly. He warned Ballmer that if there were any more serious delays, then Ballmer would be out of a job. With his company's good name threatened, Gates showed typical determination.

Microsoft goes public

One of the options available to a successful company is to "go public" and become incorporated. The company asks investors to buy shares in the company so that it is owned, in effect, by a number of different people who expect a return on the money that they have invested. To do this, the company puts its shares on the stock exchange.

In October 1985, Gates, at age thirty, began to consider this option for Microsoft. The first step in the process is to prepare a prospectus, a document that shows a realistic assessment of what the company is worth, what it owns, and a full description of its activities. The prospectus must attract the right investors. If the company does not do as well as anticipated after its launch on the stock market, then the people who launched it are liable for anything they failed to show in the prospectus. By January 1986, the Microsoft prospectus was ready.

Gates had many misgivings about going public. By law, however, when more than five hundred employees have been offered stock as a financial incentive, a company must go public. Microsoft expected to reach the magic five hundred figure sometime in 1986. That meant it had to go public. Gates was concerned that senior programmers who owned stock would begin to watch their stock investment rather than concentrate on their work. He also realized that even more of his precious time would be spent in bookkeeping.

On March 13, 1986, Microsoft was launched on the stock exchange. Because of the value of the shares

Gates (here with a former girlfriend) had little time for a social life for much of his young adult life because of his busy work schedule.

Steve Ballmer, Bill Gates's college friend from Harvard, joined Microsoft as a senior executive.

they held, Gates and Allen instantly became millionaires. By March 1987, the stock had soared in value, and Gates was officially a billionaire. His wealth was in the amount of Microsoft that he owned rather than in cash. Although his salary in 1990 was just $175,000 a year, he was now the youngest billionaire in the United States. Yet he continued to live exactly as he had before.

One thing that Gates and Allen did after their success was to pay tribute to the foresight of their old Lakeside School. They owed everything to the school that had first introduced them to the world of computers. The fact that Lakeside had made such a forward-thinking decision at the precise time that Gates and Allen were there shaped the history of the whole computing industry. Gates and Allen donated $2.2 million for a new mathematics and science building for the school. It was named the Allen Gates Hall.

Expanding

Gates had always said that he never wanted Microsoft to be a big company. He wanted to keep personal control over the whole organization and he did not want it to lose its competitive edge.

By March 1986, though, Microsoft had to move again because it now had nearly twelve hundred employees, so it purchased twenty-nine acres of undeveloped parkland just outside Seattle. Four X-shaped buildings were quickly constructed—two for the software engineers and two for everyone else. The X shape was used so that each office had a window that looked out on the leafy landscape. Each building had its own fast-food restaurant and, as always at Microsoft, all soft drinks were free.

In the middle of the four buildings was a small artificial lake, which became known as Lake Bill. Even before the complex was finished, it was too small. Within a year, the construction of more buildings began. In 1989, just three years after the move, the company bought all the parkland and had twenty-two

buildings on 260 acres; the road leading to the park was renamed "Microsoft Way."

The property had the feel of a college campus, and this was intentional. Employees were encouraged to make their offices their own—just as if they were in a dormitory. It was important to Microsoft that those who worked so hard in the pursuit of excellence should feel relaxed and at home.

Microsoft first sold shares in the company on the New York Stock Exchange (pictured) on March 13, 1986.

Success breeds enemies

By 1986, Microsoft had started to make as many enemies as friends. It had not yet come up with the updated operating system for IBM. Gates had promised IBM that Microsoft would do it, but he focused on producing Windows instead, and allowed the IBM operating system to be delayed—although he had

*Above: Drinks were
always free at Microsoft's
cafeterias because
Gates tried to make his
employees feel at home.*

*Right: Twenty years after
Microsoft was formed in a
small office, it occupied
more than two hundred
acres in Seattle—and many
other sites around the
world.*

Water, such as fountains and lakes, were added to Microsoft grounds to help create relaxing surroundings.

always been careful to back the IBM project in public. IBM was not happy when, in 1990, Windows 3.0 was released and all that Gates had claimed about his application proved to be true. This was the next stage of personal computing. IBM was lost. Anyone could buy an IBM personal computer clone and a copy of Windows 3.0, which would give them a better computer than they would have if they bought an IBM with a different operating system, such as Apple's Macintosh.

Gates had made an agreement with Apple some years earlier that Microsoft could use any advances

Apple made in its development of applications. At the time, Apple had no applications of its own and was dependent on Microsoft's. Gates knew this, and when Apple moved into applications, he incorporated Apple's advances into Microsoft products.

Apple sued Microsoft for copying. It claimed that many of the techniques used in Microsoft Windows were copies of the Apple Macintosh design. Gates's

Microsoft's headquarters was designed to have the feel of a college. Here, employees release energy from their intense work schedule on one of the company's playing fields.

determination as he defended his company's reputation is now legendary. Apple got no satisfaction from the lawsuit.

Gates was not immune to criticism and bad publicity. The sacrifices he made and his dedication made him successful. His vision and ability kept him at the top of the industry. Despite all this, he observed, "I've developed a view that being successful is not a fun thing sometimes. There is just a phenomenon where people don't like a company as successful as ours."

The FTC steps in

Despite Gates's success against Apple, it came as no surprise when the Federal Trade Commission (FTC) began an investigation in 1990. The FTC is a government agency made up of business lawyers that looks into claims that companies compete unfairly and therefore threaten the welfare of other businesses. The world of computer manufacturing has often been rife with stories of unethical activities, and Microsoft was no exception. During the investigation, Gates's rivals told several stories to illustrate how they believed

Gates had tried to steal the advantage from them. Some also claimed that he had come close to being unethical.

It was one of these stories that came to the attention of the FTC. Intuit was a relatively small California company whose business was based on a financial applications program. Gates was eager for Microsoft to produce a similar financial program.

On Microsoft's behalf, a visit was made to the chairman of Intuit, Scott Cook. Microsoft proposed to acquire Intuit and simply take it over. Cook said he was interested. After preliminary discussions, however, Gates decided the deal was too costly and withdrew. After a few months, though, Microsoft went back to Intuit to discuss the possibility that an applications program might be developed for Microsoft Windows. After the meeting, Microsoft announced that there would be no deal after all, and it would produce its own application without Intuit's help.

A little later, Microsoft launched its own financial application program, Microsoft Money. Immediately, some claimed that Microsoft had led Intuit on with promises of a deal and had used Intuit's ideas to produce its own product. The only weakness in the accusations was that Scott Cook himself said that Microsoft had done nothing wrong. Cook made it clear that Microsoft had learned nothing at Intuit.

"As far as Bill Gates is concerned, business is war," someone said at the FTC hearings. The FTC saw nothing wrong in this attitude. Many businesses are founded on such principles. The FTC acknowledged that Microsoft sold more than 100 million copies of MS-DOS. This meant that millions of Microsoft programs ran on it. It was little wonder that rivals claimed MS-DOS really stood for "Microsoft Seeks Domination Over Society."

The real testament to Bill Gates's success, however, was the move by other computer companies to try to break up Microsoft's huge business. For some time, Microsoft's rivals had complained about the company's business practices. Throughout much of the 1990s, Microsoft was investigated by the FTC and the U.S. Department of Justice.

One rival computer firm felt that Bill Gates had "kind of won fair and square," but that there was not much business left over for any other company. It was the words "kind of" that led to the FTC investigations. Many people have doubts that any one company can be so successful without bending or breaking the rules. That same rival, however, went on to give a clue to another possible explanation for Gates's success: "It's frightening to be up against him. While I'd prefer he not be in quite so much control of the world, I think that he has earned it." Whatever the opinion of Gates's competitors, the attacks on Microsoft have continued.

One of the more bizarre attempts to slow Microsoft down happened when Apple and IBM joined forces in 1991—a move that was seen as an anti-Microsoft deal. The two biggest personal computer hardware companies joined to resist the rise of a software supplier. Microsoft's dominance was obvious. Despite the efforts of others, though, in 1993, Microsoft reported its eighteenth consecutive year of growth.

Being successful

Successful business people often neglect their private lives. Bill Gates worked long hours and made time for almost nothing else. He had girlfriends, but they all knew that his work was of the utmost importance to him. His plans for a home with tunnels that connected a seven-bedroom house, banquet hall, movie screen, pool, guesthouse, and a parking area for twenty-six cars came second to his business success. It was not money, food, possessions, or pleasure that mattered—only Microsoft and its success.

Finally, though, on January 1, 1994, Gates relaxed enough to get married. At thirty-eight, America's wealthiest bachelor married one of Microsoft's managers, Melinda French, on the Hawaiian island of Lanai.

Facing the challenge

New challenges constantly face an industry where technology is always advancing, and it was Bill Gates's job to ensure that his company always stayed one step ahead of his rivals. He had to think of his customers and what they needed. In 1994, Microsoft highlighted education as the major growth area for computers and developed software packages that encouraged creativity and actual computer skills, instead of the violence and aggression of many computer games, for eight to fourteen year olds. This was a step intended to interest young computer users in a new and more socially acceptable product—surely another excellent business decision from Bill Gates and Microsoft.

Over the years, Gates and Microsoft have continued to enjoy enormous success. Improved versions of Windows, Word, and other Microsoft products are issued regularly every few years in order to keep pace with the rapidly changing needs of business and home users.

Microsoft has faced its share of challenges, too. In 1998, the U.S. Department of Justice and twenty states filed an antitrust lawsuit against Microsoft charging anticompetitive practices. In 2001, a U.S.

Opposite: Bill Gates defended Microsoft against charges that the company used unfair business practices in dealing with its competitors.

Below: At age thirty-eight, Bill Gates married Microsoft employee Melinda French.

In the mid-1990s, Microsoft developed numerous computer software applications intended to encourage and assist learning.

District Court ruled that Microsoft was in violation of antitrust law and ordered the company to break up its operations into different segments in order to make it easier for other corporations to compete. Later that year, however, Microsoft reached an agreement with the Justice Department that allowed it to avoid being broken up. The settlement was approved by a federal judge in November 2002. Although other lawsuits continue even today, thanks to his incredible judgment and drive for success, Bill Gates's Microsoft remains strong, and Gates himself remains the wealthiest man in the world.

••••••••••••••••••••••••••

". . . the computer revolution is still in its infancy—with great possibilities still in front of us."

—Bill Gates, 1993

••••••••••••••••••••••••••

Timeline

1955   October 28: William H. Gates III is born in Seattle, Washington.

1967   Bill Gates enrolls at Lakeside School.

1968   Lakeside School decides to invest in computer time for its students.

1969   Bill Gates teams up with Paul Allen and two other classmates to form the Lakeside Programmers Group.

1971   The Lakeside Programmers Group writes a payroll program for a local business, Information Sciences, Inc. This is its first real business deal.
Bill Gates goes to Harvard University, in Cambridge, Massachusetts.
December: Paul Allen sees an article about a home computer kit, the Altair 8800, in *Popular Electronics*. Allen and Gates contact Ed Roberts of MITS to say they have a form of the computer language, BASIC.

1975   February: BASIC is finished, and later in the year, Gates and Allen sign a deal with MITS.
April: Gates and Allen set up Microsoft in its own building in Albuquerque, New Mexico.

1977   January: At the age of twenty-one, Bill Gates drops out of Harvard University. Microsoft is released from its contract with MITS and owns its BASIC outright. Bill Gates and Microsoft make an agreement with Kuzuhiko Nishi for future developments in Japan.

1979   January 1: Due to the growth of the company, Microsoft moves to a new location in Seattle.

1980   Microsoft and the computer manufacturing company IBM make a deal regarding languages and operating systems for IBM's new range of personal computers.

1981   Microsoft signs a deal with Seattle Computer Products to license Q-DOS, and later buys the operating system outright. Microsoft's MS-DOS is introduced onto IBM personal computers. Bill Gates decides that Microsoft should enter the applications market.

1982   Paul Allen is diagnosed with Hodgkin's disease.

1983   For health reasons, Paul Allen decides to leave Microsoft.
April: Microsoft introduces a handheld pointer tool, the mouse.
September: Microsoft's first applications program, Word 1.0, is launched,
November: Bill Gates announces that Microsoft will launch a new way to use a computer with a graphical user interface (GUI) known as Windows.

1986   March 13: Microsoft is launched on the stock exchange; Gates and Allen become instant millionaires.
August: Bill Gates and Paul Allen donate $2.2 million to Lakeside School for a new science and mathematics building, which becomes known as the Allen Gates Hall.
With more than twelve hundred employees, Microsoft has to move again.

1990	May: Microsoft Windows 3.0 is launched to great acclaim.
	July: The Microsoft Corporation becomes the first personal computer software company to exceed over $1 billion in sales in a single year.
1992	April: Microsoft is completely successful in its lawsuit with Apple. The final judgment is made in support of Microsoft in June 1993.
1993	January: Microsoft becomes the world's largest computer-industry company based on the total value of its stock, a measure known as market value.
	March: Microsoft moves forward in the educational computer software market by announcing five new multimedia titles; each one is intended to promote the use of multimedia in education.
1994	January 1: Bill Gates marries one of Microsoft's marketing managers, Melinda French, on Lanai, Hawaii.

Glossary

applications: Programs that are specially written to make computers perform particular tasks. For example, different application packages can turn the computer into a word processor, a database, or enable it to lay out spreadsheets for accounting work.

BASIC: Beginner's All-purpose Symbolic Instruction Code is a simple and universal computer programming language. It was developed in 1964 and is very popular with amateur programmers because it is fairly easy to learn.

bug: A bug is a mistake in a computer program or system that makes the computer stop working. Some bugs cause the program to fail immediately, while others remain dormant until a certain function triggers the bug. Bugs can be introduced into a system on purpose.

clone: An exact copy of

something already in existence. In this case, it relates to copies of well-known brands of computers and computer software. IBM computers have been copied, or cloned, more than any other brand.

COBOL: Common Business-Oriented Language is a computer programming language designed for business use.

commercial: Produced with the intention of making a profit.

computer language: Any set of instructions written in a short, simplified group of words or numbers that a computer has been told to recognize through its operating system. There are several forms of computer language that different computers are programmed to understand; these include BASIC, COBOL, FORTRAN, and Pascal.

crash: When a computer program suddenly fails and stops in the middle of a

task or program.

database: An organized store of information used for computer processing.

disk: A device that stores information for computers on plates that have been coated with a magnetic layer.

entrepreneur: A person who takes risks to set up a new business in order to make a profit.

executive: A person in a position of authority within a business or company.

FORTRAN: A simple, universal computer programming language. It is very popular with scientists because it can be used to work out complicated formulas. It is short for "formula translation."

graphical user interface (GUI): A system where icons and menus are shown on a control bar on the screen of a computer. The operator uses a pointer tool, usually a mouse, to select the command needed. The system was developed to make computing easier than the complicated older method that used codes and numbers.

hacking: The activities of a computer enthusiast who uses a computer as a hobby. A hacker may also try to break into company or government computer systems to gain illegal access to secret information.

hardware: All the equipment, such as the mechanical and electronic parts of a computer, including the disk drive and the visual display unit of a personal computer.

icon: A small picture on the screen of a computer. The user can simply click on the picture, which represents a function, rather than type in a command.

incorporated (public limited company): Refers to a company formed by several owners. Each owner is responsible, by law, for only a limited amount of the company's debts.

insomniac: Someone who is unable to sleep.

IQ (intelligence quotient): A number that rates a person's mental and academic ability.

licensing: The granting of the right to use a product.

market: In terms of a company's sales plan, the number of people who might want to buy a particular item; it also means to sell the item in an organized and preplanned way.

monopoly: The domination of one company over the sales of a particular product or service, or one particular market, to the extent that it is difficult for other companies to compete. This can mean that the dominant company is able to set its own price level and keep the price unreasonably high because it is the only business that provides the product or service. There are laws against this type of monopoly.

mouse: A small, handheld device used to select the commands given to the computer. The mouse controls an arrow that appears on the computer screen and is used to point at the icon or function of the user's choice. The user clicks on the icon to activate the command.

operating system: A program of instructions stored on the computer's disk drive, or on a disk, that tells the computer how to carry out all the basic tasks it has to perform.

personal computer (PC): A small, powerful, desktop computer. The personal computer has become widely used in both the home and the workplace. The other types of computer are mainframe and minicomputers. The mainframe is a bigger computer with a huge memory capacity, and is generally used by large organizations for many operators to use at once. The minicomputer is smaller than a mainframe but bigger than the personal computer.

profit: The money that is left over in a business deal once any costs have been paid.

program: A list of instructions and codes that control the operation of a computer.

prospectus: A printed pamphlet that details the activities and achievements of a business.

royalty: A fee payable to the owner for the right to use a new invention.

share: An equal part of a company's capital (overall wealth) that can be bought and owned by a member of the company. If a person buys a share, he or she is then entitled to a percentage of the company's profits.

software: The computer programs and procedures that make the computer perform specific functions and tasks. It is necessary to have software to make a computer function.

stock exchange: The place where shares in different companies are bought and sold.

teletype: A machine that uses electronic signals to send and receive messages. When it receives a message, it converts the signal into print.

windows: A facility on later computer software programs in which a rectangular area on a computer screen displays a menu of commands or functions. A number of windows can be opened at one time. The purpose of windows is to make computers more user-friendly.

word processor: A software program designed specifically to work with text—to input, edit, and print words.

Index